For my son Rolf

*Hermit Crabs live
on the ocean floor.
Their skin is hard,
except for the abdomen,
which is soft.*

*To protect this "soft spot"
the hermit crab
borrows a shell and
makes this its "house."*

*Then only its face,
feet and claws stick out
from the shell.
That way, it can see,
walk and catch its food.*

*When a hermit crab
is threatened, it withdraws
into its shell until the
danger has passed.*

A House for Hermit Crab

HARCOURT BRACE & COMPANY
Orlando   Atlanta   Austin   Boston   San Francisco   Chicago   Dallas   New York
Toronto   London

"Time to move," said Hermit Crab one day in January.
"I've grown too big for this little shell."

He had felt safe and snug in his shell. But now it was too snug.
Hermit Crab stepped out of the shell and onto the floor of the ocean.
But it was frightening out in the open sea without a shell to hide in.

"What if a big fish comes along and attacks me?" he thought.
"I must find a new house soon."

Early in February, Hermit Crab found just the house he was looking for. It was a big shell, and strong. He moved right in, wiggling and waggling about inside it to see how it felt. It felt just right.

"But it looks so—well, so *plain*," thought Hermit Crab.

In March, Hermit Crab met some sea anemones.
They swayed gently back and forth in the water.

"How beautiful you are!" said Hermit Crab.
"Would one of you be willing to come and live on my house?
It is so plain, it needs you."

"I'll come," whispered a small sea anemone.

Gently, Hermit Crab picked it up with his claw
and put it on his shell.

In April, Hermit Crab passed a flock of starfish moving slowly along the sea floor.

"How handsome you are!" said Hermit Crab.
"Would one of you be willing to decorate my house?"

"I would," signalled a little sea star.

Carefully, Hermit Crab picked it up with his claw and put it on his house.

In May, Hermit Crab discovered some coral.
They were hard, and didn't move.

"How pretty you are!" said Hermit Crab.
"Would one of you be willing to help
make my house more beautiful?"

"I would," creaked a crusty coral.

Gingerly, Hermit Crab picked it up with his claw
and placed it on his shell.

In June, Hermit Crab came to a group of snails crawling over a rock on the ocean floor. They grazed as they went, picking up algae and bits of debris, and leaving a neat path behind them.

"How tidy and hard-working you are!" said Hermit Crab. "Would one of you be willing to come and help clean my house?"

"I would," offered one of the snails.

Happily, Hermit Crab picked it up with his claw and placed it on his shell.

In July, Hermit Crab came upon several sea urchins.
They had sharp, prickly needles.

"How fierce you look!" said Hermit Crab.
"Would one of you be willing to protect my house?"

"I would," answered a spiky sea urchin.

Gratefully, Hermit Crab picked it up with his claw
and placed it near his shell.

In August, Hermit Crab and his friends wandered into a forest of seaweed. "It's so dark here," thought Hermit Crab.
"How dim it is," murmured the sea anemone.
"How gloomy it is," whispered the starfish.
"How murky it is," complained the coral.
"I can't see!" said the snail.
"It's like nighttime!" cried the sea urchin.

In September, Hermit Crab spotted a school of lanternfish darting through the dark water.

"How bright you are!" said Hermit Crab.
"Would one of you be willing to light up our house?"

"I would," replied one lanternfish. And it swam over near the shell.

In October, Hermit Crab approached a pile of smooth pebbles.

"How sturdy you are!" said Hermit Crab.
"Would you mind if I rearranged you?"

"Not at all," answered the pebbles.

Hermit Crab picked them up one by one with his claw
and built a wall around his shell.

"Now my house is perfect!" cheered Hermit Crab.

But in November, Hermit Crab felt that his shell seemed a bit too small. Little by little, over the year, Hermit Crab had grown. Soon he would have to find another, bigger home.
But he had come to love his friends, the sea anemone, the starfish, the coral, the sea urchin, the snail, the lanternfish, and even the smooth pebbles.

"They have been so good to me," thought Hermit Crab.
"They are like a family. How can I ever leave them?"

In December, a smaller hermit crab passed by.

"I have outgrown my shell," she said.
"Would you know of a place for me?"

"I have outgrown *my* house, too," answered Hermit Crab.
"I must move on. You are welcome to live here—
 but you must promise to be good to my friends."

"I promise," said the little crab.

The following January,
Hermit Crab stepped out and the little crab moved in.

"Couldn't stay in that little shell forever,"
said Hermit Crab as he waved goodbye.

The ocean floor looked wider
than he had remembered,
but Hermit Crab wasn't afraid.
Soon he spied the perfect house–
a big, empty shell. It looked, well,
a little plain, but...

"Sponges!" he thought.
"Barnacles! Clown fish! Sand dollars! Electric eels!
   Oh, there are so many possibilities!
   I can't wait to get started!"

Sea Anemones may look like flowers, but they are soft animals (polyps) without bony skeletons. They come in many shapes and colors. With their many arms (tentacles) they catch their prey. Some specialize in attaching themselves to the shell of the hermit crab. Then they protect and camouflage the hermit crab, and, in turn, may share the hermit crab's meals. This arrangement is called symbiosis, meaning that both animals benefit from each other.

Starfish. There are many kinds of starfish. Most have five arms growing from a central disk. The mouth of a starfish is on the underside of this disk, and it has a single, simple eye on the end of each arm. With its powerful arms it can open an oyster, or hold onto a rock during a storm when the waves lash about.

Corals are somewhat similar to tiny sea anemones that build hard skeletons around themselves. Then hundreds and hundreds of them stick together, forming whole colonies. Some look like branches; others are round or disk-like. Millions upon millions fuse themselves together to build miles-long coral reefs. Some, however, live by themselves.

Snails. There are approximately 80,000 species of snails and slugs. Some live on land, others live in the sea or in lakes. Some carry a shell–their "houses"–on their backs; others have none. The shells come in many colors and shapes.

Sea Urchins. Some are fat and round, others are thin and spindly. Many have long spines (sometimes poisonous) with which they move around and dig into the mud or rocks or other places. Their mouths, with five pointed teeth, are on the underside.

Lanternfish, like fireflies, have luminous, or light-producing, spots on their bodies that light up their dark surroundings. Some lanternfish have a lantern-like organ that dangles in front of their mouths, attracting other fish which become their prey.

This edition is published by special arrangement with Picture Book
Studio, Ltd.

Grateful acknowledgment is made to Picture Book Studio, Ltd. for permission
to reprint *A House for Hermit Crab* by Eric Carle. Copyright © 1987 by Eric
Carle Corp.

Printed in México

ISBN 0-15-302144-6

2 3 4 5 6 7 8 9 10   050   97 96 95 94 93

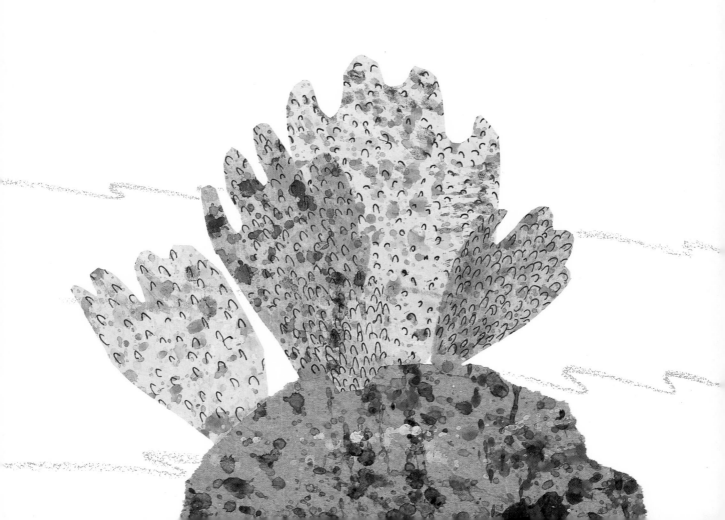

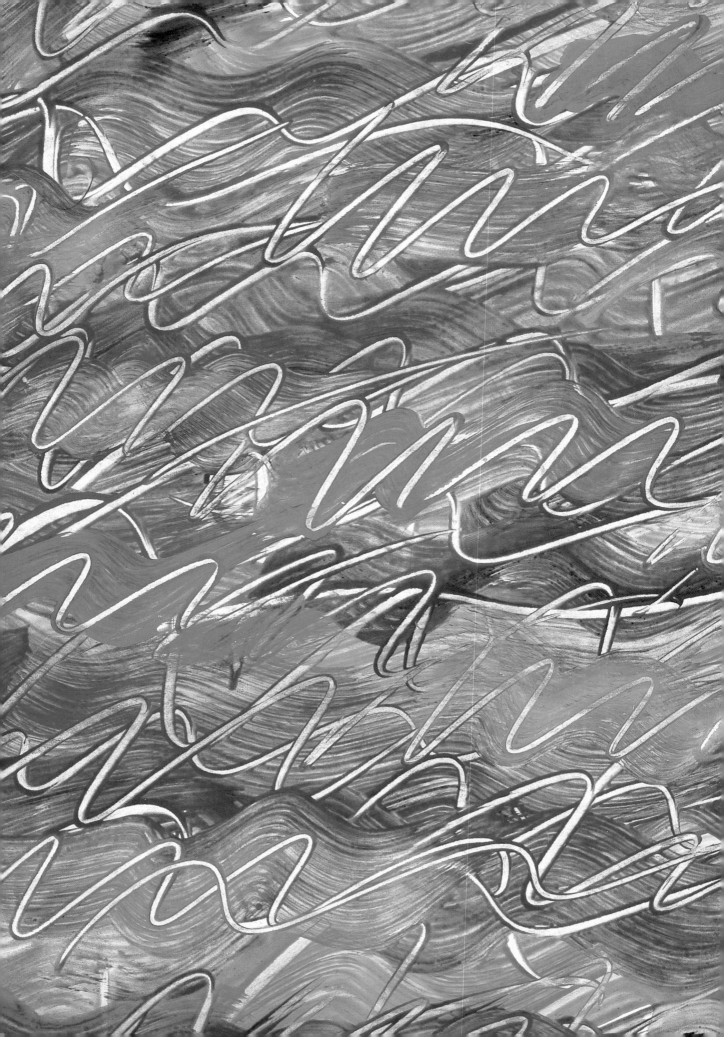